LIVING
THE
Sacred
YES

Affirmations
for
Action

Rev. Deborah L. Johnson

New Brighton Books

Copyright © 2002 by Inner Light Ministries
Cover design: Victoria May
Interior design: Nathan Walker
Printed in the U.S.A.

Library of Congress Cataloging-in-Publication Data

Johnson, Deborah L., 1956-
    Living the sacred yes : affirmations for action /
    Deborah L. Johnson.
        p. cm.
    ISBN 0-9718377-1-6 (alk. paper)
    1. Spiritual life. 2. Spirit writings. 3. Private
    revelations. I. Title.

BF1301 .J578 2002
299'.93--dc21

                                        2002033654

Table of Contents

Introduction

What we declare to be true has a powerful impact on how we think, feel, perceive, and respond. An affirmation is such a declaration of truth. It can declare not only what has been or is currently true but also what is anticipated to be true, thereby creating a mind-set for the future. We use affirmations all of the time, consciously and unconsciously. When used consciously in a positive manner—"Today is going to be a great day"—affirmations can enlighten, inspire, uplift, and sustain us. When used unconsciously, particularly in a negative manner—"This is simply going to be an impossible day"—affirmations can conspire and collude with our anxieties, fears, doubts, and self-proclaimed limitations.

The affirmations in this book are a call to action. They call us up to live the sacred Yes and together are a companion volume to the book by the same name. The sacred Yes is a place of transcendence, a place where we are in alignment with God and are aware of ourselves as spiritual beings on the path of discovering our true nature. The book *The Sacred YES* is a collection of revealed messages that teach us the principles for living in this place of transcendence in the context of our daily lives. The affirmations of *Living the Sacred YES* help us reinforce the practical application of these principles.

The flow of this book mirrors the flow of *The Sacred YES*. Like life, this flow is nonlinear, more like a spiral that keeps coming back to the same issues and principles on different levels than a step-by-step progression. The focus of the affirmations continuously shifts up and down, in and out, from the most intimate and personal to broad global concerns. The initial affirmations emphasize spiritual basics—the Universal Truths that provide a foundation for our lives. The focus then expands to personal healing and transformation; these affirmations call for us to examine our heart space and our intent for living so that we may increase our spiritual availability. Later affirmations help us to integrate Universal Truths into our daily personal practice and then into our interpersonal relationships. Finally, the affirmations towards the end of this book address issues of living in community and creating a more equitable, rewarding, and compassionate world for us all.

It is suggested that you read the affirmations to yourself out loud. The more often they are repeated, the greater the fruits they will bear in your life. The more they are repeated, the more you will be able to embody them. Work through any resistances that you may have. Resistance to spiritual affirmation is usually our small self arguing to stay small. Share these affirmations with friends or family members. The more encouragement and reinforcement you have, the better. Using these affirmations in conjunction with affirmation materials of other reputable authors and proven spiritual traditions is highly recommended.

Let the affirmations call you to action, and keep walking in the Yes.

Yes Burns in My Soul

There is a Yes burning deep within my soul. It burns within the soul of everyone. I say yes to this Yes. Forever aflame, it warms my heart and illumines my path. The Yes within me knows, and it knows that it knows. It will not collude with a sense of confusion or self-proclaimed helplessness. It transcends hesitation, reservation, and limitation. It never lets me forget that I have a purpose for being. The Yes within me reveals a vision of my greater yet to be. Too precious to squander or waste, my strength is used in the service of my vision. ∽

I Begin This Day with Yes!

I begin this day with Yes! Yes to Spirit. Yes to Life. Yes to my life as Spirit. More than an agreement, Yes is the foundation stone upon which I build my spiritual house. I live in the consciousness of Yes; it is my dwelling place. The energy of Yes goes before me and makes the rough places smooth. It beckons me out of my comfort zones. I heed its call and disturb my own inner slumber. Yes reverberates in my being, expanding my heart, my mind, and my vision. With Yes, I see more clearly what is and what is to be. ✧

I Have Unshakeable Faith

Anchored in the solid rock of Truth, I have unshakable faith. Though small as a mustard seed, my faith can move mountains. Deep in my soul I know that God is the only Source and the strength of my life. I stand on what I know. I lean on what I know. I rest in what I know. Everything about me displays confidence in the

Goodness of God's Plan. I release my attachment to doubt, worry, and fear. My choice is always to move quickly back to Center. I trust you, Spirit. With great comfort and pleasure I declare, "My life is in your hands." ✂

God's Inexhaustible Supply

Never has there been a cosmic
famine or a spiritual drought. I am
tapped into God's Inexhaustible
Supply. I don't have to beg for,
borrow, or steal my Good. I am
never forgotten, overlooked, or
ignored. The Divine Blueprint has
me in mind. My every need is
met on time and in a most perfect
manner. I am wealthy beyond

measure. My cup always overflows. My heart swells up with gratitude. I am victorious over lack, triumphant over limitation. I excel in all areas of my life. I stand on the solid rock of Truth and proclaim, "I Am that I Am." ∝

All Things Work Together for Good

The Creator of all things is equally available to each and every creation. In Spirit there is neither competition nor contradiction. Spirit is all there is, and It is never divided against Itself. The Goodness of God is benevolent and beneficial to all. In every circumstance I remember that there is a Divine Plan. The Divine Plan always culminates in a "win/win" for all because that is Spirit's deep and only intent. No longer anxious about the process of Life, I embrace the journey. I am grateful for believing and knowing that all things work together for Good. ⚬

Living a Life of Intent

Before I engage in any activity, I ask myself, "What is my deep intent?" I make certain that my intent comes from a place of Spirit, not ego. Every goal that I set reflects my deep intent. Fulfilling my intent is more sacred than accomplishing my goals. My intent speaks louder than my actions. My intent says more than my words. When my intent is pure, I am an open channel for God to express through. Blessing everything that happens, I see how all things work together for Good. I awaken to God's deep possibilities within me, which are merely awaiting my conscious embrace. ∞

Love Heals

Love is the healing agent in the universe. It is the power of the mind to unify. Love is everywhere present, equally available to all. Love is available through me. Love overcomes misunderstandings and disagreements. Love melts walls and builds bridges. Love heals all wounds. Love is neither jealous nor possessive. Love simply loves.

I allow myself to be an open channel
for love's highest expression. As pure
Spirit, my very nature is love. I give
and accept love because I am love.
I trust love with my very life.

A River of Joy
Floods My Soul

I am not joyful because of circumstances; I am joyful in spite of
circumstances. I am joyful because
I know that God, Life Itself, is Good
all of the time. Since I maintain
an attitude of gratitude, I am
constantly aware of this Goodness.
On wings of a grateful heart, I rise
above fears of separation and limitation. I keep a daily praise journal

that reminds me of the blessings of my journey. The more I give thanks, the more I realize just how much there is to be thankful for. I open the floodgates of my soul and a river of joy runs through it. ✑

I Am Spiritually Available

This day I choose to express the truth of my divine nature. No longer is my imagination limited by my experience. I stop letting the smallness of others determine the fullness of my life. I let go of the excess baggage I have been carrying around simply because it is familiar. I empty my storage bins so that the Spirit of the Living God can fall fresh on me this day. I am completely available for Spirit to express authentically in, through, and as me. I thank God for being God. I thank God for being me. I thank God that we are One. ✂

I Cultivate
Possibility Consciousness

Everything in the Universe naturally tends towards balance and equilibrium. I allow this restorative energy to permeate every aspect of my life. Possibility consciousness is continuously cultivated in my mind. I never limit what's possible to what is probable. I acknowledge facts without allowing them to define the potential of the Divine.

Seeing through appearances, I remain rooted in the Truth that I know. Living by Grace, I remain confident that Divine Order prevails. My very life is proof positive that there are miracles among us. I give thanks for the time and energy to pursue divine unfoldment in every area of my life. ∞

My Unique Reason
for Being

My existence is not a random act of fate. My being created is part of the grand Plan of the Universe. I have a unique reason for being, which makes me special in my own right. No one else sees what I see, feels what I feel, or responds as I do. No one else can create or give what I can. No one else can seize the opportunities to make a difference that are mine. Only I can express my gifts. Only I can fulfill my destiny. I am an awesome individualized expression of God. ✄

My Spiritual Truth and Personal Authenticity

Every day I am growing in awareness of my spiritual Truth and my personal authenticity. I hold both in sacred space. My spiritual Truth, being the nobler of the two, calls me up to higher levels of authentic expression. As I integrate my Truth and my authenticity in every aspect of my life, I increase my capacity to love and be loved. My relationships evolve, mirroring my expanded awareness. There is no desire to allow my heart to crystallize in any one particular state or period of time. As my heart matures, I allow my love to have its seasons and declare them all to be purposeful and Good. ☙

I Choose Love

Love lights the way, even in the darkest night. It is the soul's bridge across all troubled waters. I choose love as my attitude, love as my intent, and love as my only weapon and defense. Love heals where all else fails. Through love I overcome the desire to distance. Revenge finds no refuge in my heart. Free from shackles of separation, I celebrate my connectedness to all things. Prayer keeps me aware that I abide in love and love abides in me. The more I choose love, the more I recognize that love has already chosen me. ❧

I Know Who I Am
in Spirit

I have the patience to be kind to myself and others as we discover the Truth of who we are. I have the compassion to see the Divine in everyone, regardless of status or deed. I have the gratitude of one who appreciates countless blessings, big and small. I have the humility to ask for and accept divine guidance and direction. I have absolute trust in the Absolute and the process of divine unfoldment. I have the courage to keep walking in the direction of my surrender. I have love in my heart, peace in my soul, and a mind that rests assured. I know who I am in Spirit. ⚘

My Inner Light

Deep within me is a special place of wholeness and spiritual perfection. It is the center of my being, where I experience my Oneness with everything. It is transcendent, healing false beliefs of duality and separation. I call it my Inner Light. It shines so brightly that it warms the hearts of everyone I encounter. When lights meet each other, they merge and multiply. We are integral parts of the fires in each others' souls. ⁂

Living Beyond the Bell Curve

My expectations of what is possible are not confined to what is probable. What is probable is a snapshot of what has already happened when we rely on our own devices. What is possible is an indicator of what can happen when we trust in God's ability to do all things. I stake my claim on life in the realm of all possibility, not the realm of past experiences. I live my life fully, far beyond the assumptions and predictions of the bell curve. I am willing to be authentic, unique, one of a kind. Eyes have not seen nor ears heard of the glory that is mine in the Lord. ✀

My Body Is a Temple

My body is a temple. I treat it with
dignity and respect, honoring it for
the holy place that it is. I am the
epitome of health, full of energy
and vitality. I affirm my body's
natural healing powers and facili-
tate its healing processes. I take
care of my body and support its
natural balance. I exercise, rest, and
eat proper foods. I keep my body

free from abuse, unnecessary stress, and addictions. I am grateful for this body of mine, even for its seeming flaws. I adore this body, the dwelling place of my soul, through which I love, create, and express. ✺

Giving Myself Permission to Transform

The butterfly that makes a home of its cocoon will never fly. The seed that clings to being a seed cannot fulfill its great mission in life. I honor and appreciate the caterpillar within me and give it permission to stop being a caterpillar. I support its transforming into the butterfly that I am destined to be. I honor and appreciate the seed within me and conspire with its desire to get out of itself. I break through my own shell, anchor my roots, and blossom into full being. I harbor no regrets about relinquishing the former me so I can ascend to my Higher Purpose. I am at peace with every phase of my journey. ✢

Rich in Spirit

I am rich in the fruits of the Spirit.
I am rich in the very substance of
Life. I am an open channel for the
Divine Flow. I radiate the richness
of the soul. Regardless of my
circumstances, I continue to be a
great giver in life. My every
thought, word, and deed affirms
that I am enough. Every area of my
life demonstrates a wealth beyond

measure. I appreciate my life—
everything about my life. I give
God the honor and the glory as the
true Source of all. My coffer is
never empty because my heart is
always full. ∽

The Intent to Bless and Be Blessed

As I travel along the road of Life, I meet my intent at every step. My intent arrives before I do, setting the tone for how I experience the events of the moment. I don't just look back upon my journey, seeking God in all things after the fact. I strive to see only God while taking each step along the way. My intent is to bless and be blessed by all people, events, and circumstances. What a pleasure it is to be an active agent of healing and grace! There is a sweet harvest to be reaped from thoughts, words, and deeds sown in love. ✧

The Path of Least Resistance

I no longer choose to travel upstream, against my inner wisdom. I no longer do things the hard way just to do them my way. I move with life's ebbs and tides, resisting nothing. Like a river, I simply flow over, under, around, and through anything that appears to be in my way. I travel the path of least resistance, intact and at peace with myself and my surroundings. "Nothing in the world is as soft and yielding as water. Yet for dissolving the hard and inflexible, nothing can surpass it" (Lao-tzu). ✂

Getting Over Wanting It to Be Over

Life is an upward spiral, bringing me back to familiar places at higher and higher planes. I welcome these visitations as opportunities to experience and demonstrate my growth. Appearing to be in the same old place is an illusion that does not fool me. I gain the insights now that I wasn't ready to perceive before. Valuing the newness of this moment, I am not tempted to rush into the future. I am content to learn the lessons right where I am. I no longer ask, "How long do I have to go through this?" As I give thanks for the opportunity to experience the circumstances that deepen my faith, I ask, "Is this long enough?" ⁊

I Am Always Home

My spiritual journey is the collection of experiences and insights that reveal the innate Goodness of my nature. I release all experiences to God's redemptive Grace, allowing them to be transformed into blessings for all. I am at peace—at home with myself and my surroundings. At home, I am loved, appreciated, and protected. At home, I am nurtured, cultivated, and inspired. At home, I give, serve, and share. At home, I am free to heal and dream, to reflect and correct. At home, I simply Am, true to myself and true to my God. My life's destination is home, not merely arriving home but being home, wherever I am. ✂

The Courage and Surrender of Yes

Surrender is my embracing God's infinite possibilities more than the finite facts. I remain open to the greater possibilities that I have yet to recognize. In letting go of my need to control, I enjoy how my journey divinely unfolds. I don't have to know where I am going to know that I am headed in the right direction. As the Yes of my soul reveals itself, I am headed straight towards Grace. I have the courage to stand where I am and take the next step ahead of me. I have the courage to keep walking in the direction of my surrender. ✂

From Expectations to Expectancy

"Pain pushes until vision pulls." I do not need to be pushed into taking the action I know I must take. Things do not need to be unbearable before I give myself permission to move on. I grow and expand because I have a larger vision of my capabilities and life's potential. I go from good to better. I always receive support because I give it freely. All I need to do is believe that it can be done. Spirit will work out the details. I let go of particular expectations and move into a state of pure expectancy. I am grateful for every phase of unfoldment. ❧

Committing to the Long Haul

Life is not a series of random events. It is an ongoing process, unfolding moment by moment. I am fully present for every moment of its unfoldment. My commitment to the long haul is not merely a promise to show up later on. I am available—physically, emotionally, and spiritually—every step of the way. I do not lose the preciousness of this moment by belaboring the past or racing off into the future. I receive the gifts of each day. My life is a continuum of awe and inspiration. I claim the fullness that is awaiting my embrace. ❧

Opportunity at Every Moment

I have the opportunity at every moment to choose what I say, do, and perceive. I have the opportunity at every moment to shine, to retract, or to suspend. I never let an opportunity to shine my Inner Light pass me by. I do all of the loving, creating, sharing, and forgiving that is before me to do. I don't wait for some other time to give my gifts. By my very beingness, I am a blessing to the world and to myself. This day I am the All that I know I can be. This day I shine for the Divine. ✑

Tapped into the Source

Spirit cannot withhold Truth and never keeps secrets from Itself. One with the Source, I am tapped into the wellspring of infinite knowledge that is fully accessible to me at all times. Whenever I suspend my opinions, I discern the Truth that is before me all of the time. I refrain from gazing upon my life as a mere reflection of past experiences. I stop looking to people, places, and things to solve the riddles of my life. I turn to God's wisdom dwelling in me for guidance and counsel. All of Life's mysteries have rhyme and reason when I allow myself to see through the eyes of God. ∽

A Life in Alignment

My inner knowledge is wiser than my cognitive comprehension. I pray for the clarity to understand what I already know inside. My conscious awareness is infused with a sense of the sacred. My every act reflects reverence and spiritual intention. I allow Spirit to organize my day according to what is important. I release myself from self-imposed demands. I free myself from the tyranny of my own timetables. I yield my plans to God's priorities. My steps are guided and ordered. I give thanks for the freedom to not exercise my own will. Thank you, God, for a life in alignment with you. ❧

Accessible and Available

Thank you, Holy Spirit, for your
unwavering availability. Thank you
for modeling how to be ever present
in a relationship. I register my
intent to do my part. Regardless of
circumstances, I am accessible and
available to you. Our relationship has
my constant, undivided attention. I
listen as you speak to my heart. I
revel in your clarity, heed your

counsel, and rest in your reassurance. I commune with you every day, throughout the day. I embrace my journey, fulfilling my life's purpose, forever grateful that we walk hand in hand. How sweet is the surrender as you lead me to the waters of your living Grace. ♣

My Relationship with the Divine

Cultivating my relationship with the Divine is among my highest priorities every day. I continually reaffirm my innate goodness and allow myself to naturally gravitate towards restoration and balance. I maintain a lifestyle that supports healing and spiritual transformation. I convert all conditions into opportunities to practice the presence of God. I remember that my inner being can never be hurt, harmed, or injured. I reward myself for shifts in my perception more than I criticize myself for being where I am. I am at peace with my journey and patient with the process of living. ✃

Daily Communion

I pray every day not out of duty or habit but out of desire and intent. My daily communion with the Beloved of my soul is the sweetest and richest part of my day. I take the time to mind my mind, remembering the sovereignty of God over all conditions and circumstances. I take solace in the fact that Divine Order reigns supreme. In prayer I am uplifted, inspired, nurtured, guided, and protected. Malice melts from my heart, and I become an instrument of empowerment, transformation, and reconciliation. Through prayer I create the space for divine unfoldment and manifestation. ✂

My Soul Is Restored

The Lord is my shepherd and
I want for nothing. I am led to
green pastures and still waters.
My soul is restored. My cup runs
over with goodness and mercy.
I live not by my own might but by
the grace of God. The weight of
the world is not on my shoulders.
I don't have to figure everything
out. I know that God's Love and

Infinite Supply constantly manifest in my life. Spirit's plans for me are better than what I could create myself. I place all of my affairs in the hands of pure Spirit. With faith and confidence I lean on the Everlasting Arms. ✂

In All Things
Claim the Victory

Understanding that God is all there is, I know that nothing exists outside the realm of Spirit. There are not two worlds, the spiritual and the "real." There is only the spiritual world. It is real. And I live, move, and have my being in it. I live each day anchored in the awareness that all circumstances work together for my Good. No person, place, or thing has the power to decrease my worth or ability. Appearances don't scare me. Facts cannot shake the Truth upon which I stand. I am One with the Only thing that is, and it is never divided against itself. In all things I claim the victory. ✂

The Rhythm of My Soul

My soul has its own internal drum-beat. I have no desire to quicken its rhythm or to slow down its pace. I still myself often enough to synchronize with its vibration. My soul is in harmony with God. Everything in my life is in motion, in perfect step with the Universe. I choose my life and walk freely and consciously along my path.

Nothing within me waits for permission, recognition, or validation. Trusting my inner timing, I accord with my own being and align with the Divine. ❧

There Is Enough

My thoughts are contagious, spreading the good news that there is enough. Everything I say and do declares that there is enough. Rejoicing in my liberation from limitation, I proclaim that I am enough. I flow in a river of resources, completely engulfed in Grace. I am humbled by the sheer magnitude of Good expressing in my life. With my attitude of unconditional gratitude I consciously create the space for Good to multiply. I bless all that I have and all that is coming into manifestation. My generosity inspires those around me and leaves a rich legacy for generations to come. ✗

Unconditional Praise

Praise is an internal, spontaneous, grateful celebration of Life. I begin each day and every interaction with praise. My praise is not a response but an affirmation. The opening it creates in my awareness enables me to appreciate myself and all that is around me. I refrain from fixating on what appears to be missing. Half-empty glasses are not my reality.

I see the fullness of what's in the glass; I see the fullness of everything around me without regard to its quantity. In praise, my awareness is transcendent. I embrace the spiritual essence of all things, holding the high watch for their fullest expression. ∝

Grateful Not to Be in Control

I pray to move beyond my own perceptions. I pray to work with, not against, the Divine Plan. I maintain a self-image of being pure Spirit in the flesh. Daily I affirm that God's Goodness is at hand, equally available to all. I accept God's promise to meet my needs, not my expectations. I remain open to new possibilities. I receive mercy and compassion because I graciously extend them to others. Greater than any calamity, God transforms everything into a blessing. I am so grateful that God is in control, not me. Let Thy will, not mine, be done. ❧

Prayer Is a Movement in Consciousness

Prayer is the movement of my consciousness into alignment with Divine Order. Prayer is a refuge for the weary mind, a harbor for the heavy heart, a respite from the need to control. My prayer is the pronouncement of my readiness to see through the eyes of God. My prayer is my permission for Spirit to transform my thoughts and feelings.

No longer focused on facts and probability, I embrace Truth and possibility. My faith is strengthened through prayer, and my trust is renewed. Prayer gives me the courage to keep on keeping on. When I pray, I know in my soul that all is well. ✂

Answered Prayer

Prayer is the movement of my consciousness through the field of all possibility. This field neither comes nor goes but remains ever steadfast. Prayer dislodges me from where I've been stuck on my treadmill. Releasing my own plan, I become a place for the manifestation of the Divine Plan. Fear subsides, anger dissipates, and the fog of confusion lifts. Through prayer I appreciate the moment and find the strength to carry on. The answer to my prayer is the healing and the transformation I undergo as part of the process of unfoldment. I surrender to the answer to my prayer, forever grateful for each chance to change. ❧

Thank You for Being in My Life

Everyone and everything that comes into my life bears a gift for me, and I for them. Although not always quickly discerned, the gift reveals itself to me as I open up to its possibility. I do not allow the inner sanctum of my heart and mind to be disturbed by the energy of resistance or resentment. I am at perfect peace with myself and my surroundings. I give thanks to the people, places, and things that have created the context for my divine insights. My journey is a fascinating combination of people and events. I bless them all for being wonderful catalysts and mirrors of consciousness. To everything and everyone I say, "Thank you, for being in my life." ❧

Healing All Separation

The only thing that ever needs to be healed is the sense of separation. Love is the power that heals all separation. I am committed to healing separation through the energy of my love. Like branches on the same tree, we all share the same Life. You are some manifestation of me, and I of you. I am mindful that everything that I do and say to you rebounds back on me. I choose my words carefully, making certain that they bless and bring us both closer to God. I am deliberate in my actions, seizing every opportunity to encourage and uplift. Never fooled by appearances, I know that there is only One of us here. ❧

Mirrors and Reflections of Each Other

There is only One Life, One Power, One Essence. It expresses as each and every one of us. We all live in the same energy field. We all love with the same heart, think with the same mind. We exist only because we are connected to the whole. Individually, we are distinct expressions but not separate entities. Any sense of separation or otherness is an illusion. You are a representation of me and I of you. We are mirrors and reflections of each other. I can't do anything to you without it reciprocating on me. There is only One of us here. ✿

The Intent to Love

This day, I will the love within me, the love that I am, to express. I give it shape and form, allowing it to flow to and from me without regard to its being deserved or earned. I love because my nature is One with everything. I deliberately choose to love, even when I do not feel like loving. As my judgments subside, my inaccessible heart space becomes available. I take down my barriers, disrobe from my armor, and stand in the nakedness of Truth. The floodgates of my heart are open wide. I love my enemies. I love my neighbors as myself. I love the Lord, my God, with all my heart, with all my soul, with all of my mind. ∝

No Need to Formulate an Opinion

It is not necessary for me to formulate a personal opinion about everybody and everything. I transcend the temptation to express one, especially in matters that don't concern me. I stop speculating about what is in the hearts and minds of others. "There are at least two sides to every story, and then there is the Truth." I am only concerned with the Truth, which is void of opinion. Spirit will reveal to me whatever I need to know. I begin each inquiry into what has happened with the premise that all things work together for Good. My thoughts, words, and deeds are infused with the healing energy of compassion. ⌀

Our Indwelling Christ

There is a Christ Consciousness that dwells in each and every one of us. It is our awareness of ourselves as spiritual beings—perfect, whole, and complete. It can be neither created nor destroyed, only revealed. Our indwelling Christ is pure and intrinsic. The heart is its womb and incubator. Never stagnant or stale, it is always fresh and genuine.

Our indwelling Christ is fully present, redeeming each moment in Oneness and Love. The Christ in me affirms and supports the Christ in you. Together we are a mirror unto the world that says, "Look at how beautiful Life in Truth can be." ⸕

I Salute the Divine in You

In your eyes I recognize the truth, beauty, and power of pure Spirit. I know who you are beyond what you have done. I know who you are beyond what has happened to you. I see your Essence, and it is magnificent. I see it in you because it resonates in me. One Heart, One Love, One Life, One Spirit. To salute is to acknowledge rank and authority. I salute the Divine in you. I salute the Divine in us all. It is worthy of honor, recognition, and praise.

Letting Go of the Past

I am greater than the sum total of all of my experiences. My past does not hold onto me, and I don't hold onto it. I forgive myself for anything I did when I forgot who I was in Spirit. As I extend this same compassion to others, they give it back to me. We free each other from the rippling effects of past consciousness. Only Spirit can bring clarity and peace. Only Spirit can right the wrongs. Being neither judge nor jury, I release the process of correction to the capable hands of God. Thank you, Spirit, for helping me to view everything through fresh new eyes. ∽

As We Forgive
Our Debtors

Forgiveness is the release of judgments about ourselves and others. Forgiveness does not condone, erase, or let anyone off the hook. By separating the action from the actor, it breaks the hypnotic suggestion that we are our "stuff." Forgiveness unleashes the blessing in all situations and creates the space for everything involved to be spiritually transformed. An act of compassion, forgiveness energetically clears the way for healing and restoration. As I forgive others their transgressions, I am freed from the psychological bondage of my own. I willingly give myself and others the profound gift of forgiveness. ✂

Scripts in Each Others' Lives

The script that I write for you is what needs fulfillment in me. I release you from the responsibility of making my life work, and I never assume that responsibility in yours. I let go of the script that casts us as victim and villain. Although each of us can play either, in truth we are neither. We consciously choose to resonate with each other's power more than our pain. You are only as kind and patient with me as I am with myself. I love you only as unconditionally as I love myself. Relationships are a divine laboratory. I show up each day, ready for and appreciative of all that I learn. ❧

Drama Is Optional

I would rather focus on Truth than on a juicy story. I refrain from gossip and conjecture. I never fabricate to enhance facts. I don't speculate to complete a story. Spiritual clarity is more important than my ego's need to know. Since I patiently await divine unfoldment, I always know what I need to know when I need to know it. I am an instrument of divine justice beyond judgment. I offer Christ Consciousness, not criticism. My words uplift and inspire. My love brings more resolution than my opinion. Drama is optional, and I pass on the option. I stay centered and focused no matter what. ✂

My Responsibility to Make Choices

I have a vested interest in my community, in my nation, and in the world. I am a full-fledged citizen of them all. My every thought, word, and deed has an impact on those around me and leaves a legacy for those who will follow. I never underestimate the importance of my existence. I am fully aware of my power to either create change or support the status quo. I accept my personal and collective responsibility to make choices about how society is ordered and governed. I use my time, my resources, and my voice to make the world a better place in which to live. This day I support the individuals and organizations that empower all people to be their highest spiritual selves. ∾

When Ideas Are Shared

The more an idea is shared, the greater is its realm of expression. The thoughts I think do not belong to me exclusively. My every thought fuels the collective consciousness. The vibration I set into motion impacts others as well as myself. Since harboring an idea is enough to bring it into manifestation, I am vigilant over the ideas that hold my attention. I join the conspiracy of thoughts holding the space for the unfoldment of the Divine. I choose to align with the vibratory patterns that support well-being. I am an instigator of goodwill everywhere I go, and I vow to be a part of creating heaven right here on earth.

Together We Can Move Mountains

At every moment we align with some idea. Every thought met in agreement is magnified. Every thought met in excessive disagreement is equally magnified. Since what we think about we bring about, we have a collective responsibility to mind our minds. Limitation is never put forth as our starting assumption or our final answer.

We make certain not to feed lack and starve abundance. Through generosity and circulation of our resources we create a global feast where everyone is welcome and all are fed. Collectively, we can do great things. Together we can move mountains. ✂

Taking the Time to Feel, Deal, and Heal

Our actions reflect our awareness of ourselves as spiritual beings. They indicate the Truth that we do or do not know. Energetically, we resonate with ideas that we share. Our individual thoughts create scripts in the drama of life in which we all participate. The most vulnerable among us acts out what the rest of us harbor in our hearts.

What we refuse to look at in ourselves we project onto others. The action of any one of us reflects some aspect of all of us. As I assume the responsibility to mind my own mind I take the time to feel, deal, and heal. ⌘

Peace Comes from Within

My sense of peace is not based on external conditions and circumstances. It is not contingent upon what others are doing in their lives or what I think they are doing in mine. Peace always comes from within. I know who I am in Spirit, and I choose a life that reflects that. Remembering the Truth, that I am One with God, always brings me back to Center. Being at peace with myself, I naturally transcend conflict and restlessness. Even in the midst of chaos and confusion I am an ambassador of peace. My very presence facilitates reconciliation and goodwill. Let the peace on earth begin with me. ∽

Moments of High Resolve

There are moments in my life when my awareness and understanding spur me on to higher levels of commitment. These are my moments of high resolve. Regardless of what happens in life, I am able to keep the intent of my resolutions in the forefront of my mind. I am clear and steadfast. I have the courage to step out on my spiritual understanding.

I consistently follow through on my commitments. I yield my ego-based decisions to the higher purpose of Divine Order. My moments of high resolve are always kept fresh before me. ∞

Thank You for My Journey

Today is the culmination of my entire life experience. My life has been filled with joys and sorrows, triumphs and tragedies—all part of being human. I bless every event in my life, knowing that love turns everything into an agent of redemption. I embrace all of me, finding strength in what I have grown to understand. I am grateful for all lessons, no matter how much I may have resisted them at the time. I love who I am and wouldn't trade being who I am for all of the world. Thank you, Spirit, for the privilege of my journey. ∽

The affirmations in this book are a tool provided by Inner Light Ministries of Santa Cruz, California. These affirmations have appeared in the Sunday Service programs as a teaching aid for sermons by Reverend Deborah Johnson that have been inspired by letters in *The Sacred YES*. These Sunday talks, available on audio cassette tapes, expand upon both the affirmations and the letters, providing living examples of their principles in practice. As an additional reinforcement, highly recommended is the "Rise Above" CD by Valerie Joi for which Reverend Johnson is a coproducer and lyricist. All are available at www.innerlightministries.com.

TITLES OF RELATED INTEREST
BY NEW BRIGHTON BOOKS

Letters from the Infinite, Vol. I
The Sacred Yes

Rev. Deborah L. Johnson

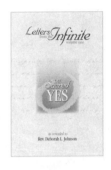

These messages, revealed to Rev. Deborah L. Johnson, provide a road map to new ways of thinking and perceiving that shifts the way in which we relate to our own selves, to each other, and to the world around us. Filled with insight and practical application, they reveal the steps necessary to reconcile our humanity with our spiritual nature. Acknowledging human frailty, resistance, and confusion, they chide, motivate, encourage, and carry us across the threshold of our great yet to be.

$19.95 • PAPER • 6 x 9 • ISBN 0-9718377-0-8

Rise Above

Valerie Joi

This CD is a sweet, soulful, spiritual journey of healing and transformation. Through the rhythms of jazz, gospel, and R&B, you are encouraged to rise above your challenges and explore your own personal relationship with the Divine. Valerie Joi is the composer and arranger on all songs. Rev. Deborah Johnson is the lyricist on several songs and co-producer of the project.

$15.00 • © 2002 TRUJOI MUSIC

We hope you enjoyed this New Brighton Books title. If you would like to receive information about additional New Brighton books and products please contact:

New Brighton Books
P.O. Box 1674
Aptos, CA 95001-1674

www.newbrightonbooks.com

To place an order call toll free
800-919-1779